START-UP LESSONS
LEARNED
ALONG THE WAY

OUR SOURCEDAY JOURNEY

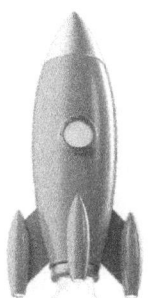

TOM KIELEY & CLINT McREE

START-UP LESSONS LEARNED ALONG THE WAY
Copyright © 2023 SourceDay

All rights reserved. No part of this book may be reproduced or transmitted in any form or by any means, electronic storage, and retrieval system, except in the case of brief quotations embodied in critical articles or reviews, without permission in writing from the publisher. For permission, please contact the publisher via contact@sourceday.com

ISBN (hardcover): 979-8-9876815-0-3
ISBN (paperback): 979-8-9876815-1-0
ISBN (ebook): 979-8-9876815-2-7

Cover & Divider Designs: Jason Stone
Page Design & Production: Domini Dragoone, Sage Folio Creative
Author Photos: SourceDay
Back Cover Photo: Jim Stone

Published by
SourceDay
Twitter: @SourceDay
LinkedIn: linkedin.com/company/sourceday-com
YouTube: @SourceDayTube

SourceDay
STOP SUPPLIER MISSES

CONTENTS

Foreword vii

PART 1: TOM KIELEY

1 ▪ Yin and Yang 1
2 ▪ The Godfather and the Gatekeeper 7
3 ▪ Flying High 11
4 ▪ Nerf Guns and Flying Cars 19
5 ▪ It's Not Impossible 27
6 ▪ Unsung Heroes 33
7 ▪ The Best Laid Plans 39
8 ▪ Early-Stage People 45
9 ▪ The Solidarity of Success 51
10 ▪ Transcending the Workplace (Giving Back) 55
11 ▪ The Tale of Two Pitches 59

A Timeline 65

PART 2: CLINT McREE

1 ▪ My Restless Entrepreneurial Mind 75

2 ▪ Things That Matter 85

3 ▪ It Doesn't Work 91

4 ▪ T-shirts and Sport Coats 95

5 ▪ The Best of Both Worlds 101

6 ▪ The Enigmatic Connectivity of Being Me 109

Epilogue 115

About Tom and Clint 118

FOREWORD

Our initial plan was to collaborate on a book about our shared SourceDay startup experience. We sat down and contemplated the blank pages of our lives. Fortunately, an epiphany followed: *Before we can even consider writing about our together SourceDay journey, we each need to process and understand our separate journeys.*

In the end, we concluded that it would be more productive if we went our separate literary ways. We agreed to meet again after completing our individual stories. Perhaps, then, we could create a book that would be a collective success.

Before parting we penciled out some commonalities to include in our separate stories:

1. Use quotations from influencers to transcend the content.
2. Avoid pontification; instead, each of us would think about and write about the lessons we have learned along the way on our SourceDay journey.
3. Tell stories.
4. Include our "perspective" at the end of each chapter.
5. Have engaging chapter titles.
6. Include the people that matter to us.

After completing our stories, we honored our previous agreement and met to discuss format, style, and purpose. A few "purpose" questions arose:

- Who are we targeting?
- Is there enough purpose and meaning layered into our stories?
- Are we educating the market on a large scale that SourceDay is the solution to their decades old and ignored challenges?

The above questions and the subsequent discussion focused our purpose: Our SourceDay Journey is *not* written to educate the market; instead, we wrote it to tell our stories of self-discovery, of "lessons learned along the way." Ironically, telling our story might be the best way to educate the market about what we do. Perhaps if a prospective customer or investor reads about our struggles, our successes, and the people that mean so much to us in our personal and professional lives, they will want to become part of our narrative. The details of what we do at SourceDay are in the book. They are subtle, but they are there.

If, however, our audience is limited to SourceDay enthusiasts: employees, partners, customers, family, and friends who want to know a little more about our character, about our families, and about our journey, then that is okay too.

The stories contained within reveal who we are both personally and professionally. Whoever you are, dear reader, we hope you enjoy it. We would like to leave you with an apropos quote from Nietzsche:

"That which does not kill us makes us stronger."

START-UP LESSONS LEARNED ALONG THE WAY:
OUR SOURCEDAY JOURNEY

"We're Partners. We are Partners."

—LETHAL WEAPON, 1987

PART 1

TOM KIELEY
CEO & CO-FOUNDER

TOM'S DEDICATION:

Dedicated to Autumn,
our three incredible kids,
and my parents for enabling me
to chase my dreams.

CHAPTER 1
YIN AND YANG

> **LESSSON LEARNED:**
> Find the right partner.

"We're Partners. We are Partners."
—*Lethal Weapon,* 1987

My first day at Pervasive Software was worrisome. I was hired to sell enterprise software, but there I was, at the helm of a purple Malibu speeding across Lake Travis, beautiful homes and lush vegetation a blur on all sides, questing for every boater's Nirvana: open water "glass". Behind the boat was colleague and future friend Clint McRee. He was casually performing flawless forward somersaults, backflips, and side rolls on his hydrofoil.

I was big into wakeboarding and, with years of boating experience, I volunteered to drive his boat because no one else knew how. Hanging out all day on the lake was fun, but I wondered if

I had made a mistake signing on with Pervasive. Did they party on barges and drink beer all the time? I can laugh about it now.

Boating was the first thing that connected us; it would not be the last.

"I think this is the beginning of a beautiful friendship."
—*Casablanca,* 1943

In Austin the next morning, July 2012, I looked up from my "Cube City" desk at Pervasive to see the hydrofoil expert who I had met yesterday sitting directly across from me. He, too, was selling enterprise software.

I soon discovered that Clint, like me, was an "outside the realm of possibility" thinker. Many of our initial conversations were about our business aspirations. Clint shared his idea for a reverse IT auction marketplace for buying hardware, and I shared my RightGift start-up story. How I had created it in 2008 before Amazon Gift Registry and before all the in-store registries existed. This was when the first iPhone dropped.

RightGift was developed as a free web App where users could create a registry for baby showers, bridal showers, birthdays, and graduations from any store or website. I shared how RightGift found its market with bridal showers and baby showers.

In another conversation, I told Clint that I had hired a back-end engineer in Bangladesh, Mehedi (we call him The Godfather) and a front-end designer, Kyle Kothe. I told Clint that I was spending most of my nights and weekends working on RightGift. My dream was to make it my career.

PART 1: TOM KIELEY'S STORIES

"It's so easy to fall in love, but hard to find someone who will catch you."
—Anonymous

Unfortunately, because of kids, bills, and the daily hustle, RightGift never came to be. I spent tens of thousands of dollars of my own money and borrowed money and over-built the platform. It seemed that customers only wanted simple registries and wish lists to share with friends and family. I ended up with maybe four or five thousand users, not nearly enough for my purposes. I was up to my eyeballs in credit card debt. It was my wife who set me straight. "I support you 100%, but we can't put any more money into this because there isn't any," she said.

But now I had met Clint and his supply chain idea. And when he asked, "Do you want to be partners?" I jumped at the idea.

"Yes!" I said. "Man, I love supply chain. Studied it in college at Texas A&M. Let's go build it."

And we did. We repurposed the early core platform of RightGift and built off that to create SourceDay.

Well sort of...

In 2013, Clint and I launched BIDSmash, LLC. It was intended to be a reverse IT auction marketplace for hardware. Companies could submit a request for laptops, monitors, keyboards, servers, hardware, or whatever IT equipment they needed.

We initially built the product as a form of RFQ (Request for Quote). When we talked to customers, however, they said, "Your product is great, but there is a problem. Our most critical challenge is PO (Purchase Order) collaboration. And PO collaboration is about meeting our existing real-time purchase order demand and about receiving our shipments faster and more on time."

After much debate, we listened to our target market, and, like many start-ups, we pivoted. Clint and I are good listeners and problem solvers. You must be when you own a startup. It's one of the many things we have in common. We agreed that the PO collaboration problem needed to be solved, so we launched phase two.

But the name BIDSmash didn't fit our new business model. We brainstormed different company names for many weeks on a whiteboard and finally agreed on SourceDay because our company is about sourcing (procuring) parts and materials every single day of the week. And it must be done without fail.

In Retrospect

When you're boating on Lake Travis or in a cubicle at work, you need a good partner. But if you're going to build a business at the scale we envisioned for SourceDay, you need a great one. Going it alone is not only challenging but foolish. You need to have someone to bounce ideas off, someone that you can trust, and someone who will share the workload. You need a partner that will be the yin to your yang.

Clint and I are very different in some ways, and that is a good thing. I'm very much the optimist, glass half full. We had a marketing person early on who called Clint, Mr. Glass Half Empty. His reply, "I'm a realist. I'm just looking at this pragmatically."

When an issue arises, I will say, "Everything is good. Anything can be done. Let's go do it."

Clint's response will be, "Here's why it can't be done. Here are the things we need to be thinking about."

PART 1: TOM KIELEY'S STORIES

There is nothing negative about either persona. It is a delicate balance. With RightGift, I had the glass half full mentality—to a fault. I tried to do everything myself. I overbuilt the product, overspent, and didn't ask for feedback from the users or the customers.

At SourceDay, we still make mistakes, but we make fewer mistakes because Clint and I are constantly questioning each other about the right direction for the company. At RightGift, I was just going blindly forward without really talking to anyone.

PERSPECTIVE: I am very fortunate for two reasons: I married the love of my life, and then I found the perfect business partner in Clint.

NOTE: As for RightGift, it is up and running. I own a minority share. I'm on the board. A CEO bought the majority share, and the business is thriving. It has become a Benefit Corporation that provides, among other things, housing for battered women who need everything from dishes to appliances in their new homes. Through RightGift, donors give to a cause. I'm so thankful that one can stumble into opportunities through bad ideas. I am thankful that Right-Gift is making a difference in the world.

CHAPTER 2
THE GODFATHER AND THE GATEKEEPER

> **LESSSON LEARNED:**
> Seek out a skilled, caring developer and find the quintessential quality automation engineer.

> "The strength of a family, like the strength of an army, lies in its loyalty to each other."
> —Don Vito Corleone, *The Godfather*, 1972

The Skilled Developer

Mehedi was the original developer for RightGift, my first startup company. I connected with him through the Bangladesh based company where he worked. The outsourced development company was owned by a local Cedar Park, Texas entrepreneur that I knew.

Mehedi and I had a *Sleepless in Seattle*, Meg Ryan-Tom Hanks kind of relationship. I say that because, despite working together 4–7 days a week, it was six years before we met in person.

Sleepless in Austin

Mehedi and I started working together in 2009, and, because of the Bangladesh/Texas time difference, it was always between the hours of 10:00 PM to 4:00 AM (CST). I worked with Mehedi over Skype: no video, just chat. I would send him an ideation for RightGift, and he would send me the compiled build of the product to test and iterate. He and I communicated anywhere from four to seven days a week for four years.

So, when we launched SourceDay (initially BIDSmash), I knew that Mehedi was the programmer I wanted. I called Mehedi. "We have a new idea. My partner Clint and I are going to build something different," I said. Mehedi had built a lot of software for many different start-up companies worldwide. I knew he would be the perfect fit.

We started working directly with Mehedi in 2013. He built the original platform from the ground up, starting with some of the base code that he had developed for RightGift. And, yes, I was still sleepless in Austin. From 2013 to mid-2015, from 10:00 PM to 4:00 AM every night, I Skyped with Mehedi. I had to. SourceDay was a much bigger platform compared to RightGift. It was enterprise, business to business, class type software which required a lot of iterating. We developed the software for two years before we launched it.

PART 1: TOM KIELEY'S STORIES

Coming to America

In 2014, Mehedi was vacationing in the U.S. so, when he arrived in Houston, he called me. "I'm only three hours away. I've got to come meet you in person," he said. We met in downtown Austin and had lunch together. After nearly ten years, we finally met in person. Our lunch together was a brief moment in time, but it brought us immeasurably closer.

The Godfather

We call Mehedi The Godfather because he is our Don Corleone behind the scenes. He always knows what to do, despite the many iterations and constant changes. "Go fast on these things. We need them by tomorrow." Mehedi always delivers. He is resilient and resolved and believes in what we are building.

Mehedi has worked on many projects in his career, but very few of his clients have built the kind of relationship that we have with him. With other clients, he usually gets a feature list or a product road map and builds the software. After he sends it back to the customer, in most instances, they never speak again. It is a business-only relationship.

During one of our late-night rendezvous, Mehedi said to me, "Tom, you're different. Unlike the other people I work with, I have a relationship with you. We started with RightGift, and now we're working together on SourceDay. We are like family."

Mehedi is right. We are like family. We were working seven days a week, nights and weekends to iterate and program our SourceDay product. Mehedi was our sole developer for two years. The product vision came from Clint and me, but the development was the work of The Godfather. It is a deserving name. And we are forever grateful.

In 2017, The Godfather moved to America. He called me when he arrived: "Good news. I'm getting married," he said. Mehedi and his wife now live in Austin, and they have a young son. We made him an offer he couldn't refuse: The Godfather now works for us full time. Mehedi and his family are now part of our family.

The Quintessential Quality Automation Engineer

Programming software is complicated. When changes are made, there are almost always unintended consequences. For us, it's critical that The Godfather spends all his time developing. But, when he compiles the code into a new release, he needs someone to run a full automation test or manual test of the platform before it is put into production. This is done to make sure there are no leaks or bugs, or other issues.

Enter The Gatekeeper

As our platform grew, it became a monolithic application. A monolithic platform is complex because it integrates several functions. Making a change in one function can have unintended consequences for another. It requires someone who says, "Nothing gets into production without going first through me." Hector Morales is that someone. He is The Gatekeeper. He makes sure that few, if any, bugs get into production and impact a customer. He is the one who tests The Godfather's code before we put it into production. With Hector, we rarely, if ever, have platform concerns.

PERSPECTIVE: Hector and Mehedi are valuable members of our SourceDay family.

CHAPTER 3
FLYING HIGH

> **LESSSON LEARNED:**
> Hire slow, fire fast.
> Develop future leaders.

> "No amount of sales, marketing, neatly crafted core values or previous success can overcome incompetent leadership."
> —Kirk Dando

In 2020, we started a project to separate and rebuild our front-end UI/UX (user experience design/user interface design) interface. From our perspective, it was a success. Our new platform increased development speed, and our user interface was cleaner and much easier to enhance and use. It created more configurability for customers, and, long term, it made for a better user experience. It was a massive uplift. It took over 12 months to build.

The bad news?

When we released our platform, because of an email screw-up, we neglected to tell all of the users of one of our largest customers about the platform change. Normally, we give two to four weeks of visual and video training for said change. "Here's what's coming. Here's what's changing."

Unfortunately, we had trained only 60% of our customers for the new release. It may seem like a minor issue, but when customers depend on your platform for their day-to-day operations, it is as major as it gets. When they logged in, everything had changed. They no longer knew how to manage their change orders or how to communicate with their suppliers. Imagine the customer waking up to a completely different system, and they had no idea that it was coming. Because of our mistake, they were helpless.

Enter Bob Pojman, our Chief Customer Officer

As soon as we realized our error, Bob and his team called every customer and executive that we had neglected to inform. He took responsibility for the communication failure and offered real-time training (and whatever else they needed) to get the customer comfortable with the new interface.

Bob worked nights and weekends with his team communicating with everyone that we missed. "This is my responsibility. I own customer success and I own customer enablement," he said. Without complaints or finger pointing, Bob solved the problem.

He is a team leader, especially when customers are angry or unhappy, or uncomfortable with something that we have done. He is the first to say, "Let me face the firing squad. Let me take the bullet for the team. And let's learn from our mistakes."

Bob is the quintessential servant leader. He is currently spearheading a six-month leadership management training program for current and future leaders at SourceDay. It is not part of his job description, but he recognizes how important building future leaders is to our company and the culture of our business.

Whether an employee stays at SourceDay or chooses to further his or her career elsewhere, we want to be part of their path to career success. We strive to hire great people who want to further their careers with us, but if they move on to bigger and better roles, we are proud to have helped them on their journey. Regardless of the path the journey takes, being able to provide opportunities internally is critical. And Bob has been leading us down that path in his spare time.

Avoid Crash Landings

For a startup company to get off the ground, the founders must have a vision. There's an old start-up saying: "You gotta build it while you're flying it." If you're a founder, you've got to build the engine, assemble the wings, and attach the landing gear while you're in the air. And you need to prepare yourself for a crash landing: no parachutes allowed.

And that design-and-build resolve must exist in the core of the people that you hire. If not, they'll be fine-tuning your blueprints all the way to the crash site.

One such hire, assigned to a key role, took our innovation to a screeching halt.

Our integration middleware connects SourceDay with its customers. One former employee built an integration platform so overly complex that it had to be scrapped. No one, not even he, could figure out how it worked or how to finish it. We had to start over. It took nine months to get one of our largest customers live. And they were none too happy.

That is just one example of several of this former employee's projects that were great ideas but which never came to be. We spent a lot of development time and resources fixing his mistakes.

This same former employee also struggled hiring A-players for our startup, go-fast culture. One such hire was in DevOps. This new employee's job was to manage our SaaS (Software as a Service) Cloud infrastructure, and our AWS hosting services. Somehow, he managed to get through the interview process, but we soon discovered that he knew nothing about DevOps. For example, one day, while I was working with him, he Googled "get hub", instead of "GitHub". It wasn't a typo. And we think he was living in our office building. Ready the Emergency Response Team. Contact the NTSB. Mayday. We're going down. He was fired immediately.

Trust Ya' Gut

> "I actually feel most at home when I find people who make me feel really dumb, who are brilliant at their particular things. And then I gather these people, put them in a room, and watch incredible things come out of it."
> —Mick Ebeling

I have learned to hire people who are exponentially smarter than me. If I'm afraid of hiring someone smarter than me, afraid they're going to take my job, then I am probably in the wrong role. My mantra is "Hire with no ego, but don't neglect due diligence."

If a prospective hire gives me a reference, that reference isn't going to say anything bad about him or her. I backchannel to find someone else to speak to. I strive to find a former boss or colleague, someone that is going to give an objective assessment and constructive feedback about a potential hire.

I've also learned the importance of interacting with prospective hires in public settings. I get a glimpse into the core of a potential hire by watching them interact with staff at restaurants, or by riding in the car with them. How they treat people is the essence.

I hired two people early-on who I thought were very capable. On paper, they appeared to be talented, intelligent people, but my intuition told me the culture fit would be toxic. It was their tone and attitude; I could see and feel it.

In their defense, they had recently worked for a large company. It's hard for people who come from a large organization like IBM or a consulting organization to succeed in an early-stage company. They must manage the fast pace and deal with ambiguity. There is constant change. In one instance, I let it play out for several months, and the situation became toxic.

"We need to cross our t's and dot our i's before moving forward," and "This is not how it should be done," and "I'm not responsible if this fails," were this individual's common refrains.

People who don't want to improve the world, who don't want to disrupt the work environment in a constructive way, and, especially who are just chasing monetary gains, are going to fail. Their decisions are going to be short-term, designed for their short-term success.

I've seen it in other companies. I've read about it and studied it. I've learned that we need to run our business long term.

SourceDay's motto, Be the Best (#BtheB) means that our strategy is to make SourceDay the best that it can be.

A Shoutout to My Co-Pilot

My father, Ken Kieley, was our first investor and has been my sounding board since I launched my first start-up, RightGift. He and I have annoyed our family and friends for the last decade by spending every dinner, holiday and family event talking strategy about RightGift and, more recently, SourceDay.

Having my father's startup, financial planning and analysis experience has been instrumental in keeping our growth sustainable. Without strong financial planning, you are building the airplane in the air without a fuel gauge, not knowing when your engines will sputter and die.

> **NOTE:** My father's nickname is Happy. It came from Bob Pojman who worked with my father several startups prior. Why "Happy"? In an ironic twist, Bob created the nickname because, when my father was the CFO, his REF (resting executive face) was a scowl.
>
> Employees were hesitant, and sometimes even unwilling, to ask Happy for the budget to buy a new tool or make a hire. With REF on full display, my father would challenge their budget ideas and convince his employees that they didn't need the added spend. His "happy" spend mentality still exists today as our fractional CFO.

PART 1: TOM KIELEY'S STORIES

EPIPHANY: Perhaps the apple doesn't fall too far from the tree.

Four Perspectives

1. A wrong hire is damaging to the business. I'm learning to go with my gut. I'm learning to listen to myself and trust my intuitions.
2. They call it "launching a start-up" because every day it feels like you're strapping onto a rocket, and you don't know where the rocket is going, and it might crash. In some cases, it does crash. In order to survive the crash, you must figure out what broke and how to repair it. You must make it better for tomorrow.
3. A servant leader needs to build the team who can build the plane in flight, ride the rocket, and take a bullet, all the while enabling others to BeTheBest.
4. One never tires of aeronautic metaphors.

CHAPTER 4
NERF GUNS AND FLYING CARS

> **LESSSON LEARNED:**
> Develop and nurture a positive "warehouse" culture.

> "Our relationship with bosses, direct reports, peers, customers, and vendors are what contribute to a meaningful workplace. More specifically, when we give and receive empathy and trust, we feel good about ourselves and our place within the organization. We relish being part of a culture that fosters these qualities."
>
> —Rishad Tobaccowala, *Restoring the Soul of Business*

In 2004, after graduating from Texas A&M with a BS in Industrial Distribution Engineering, I was hired as a 2nd shift boxing line supervisor at Dell. I oversaw anywhere from 30 to 60 employees who were, in most cases, twice my age. We worked the 4:00 PM-to-Whenever shift, four to seven days a week, depending on the workload.

I was a wet-behind-the-ears kid and managing people who, in some cases, had been working at Dell since the late 1980's. I had many questions. How do I earn their trust? How do I earn their respect? How do I build a team? How do I build comradery? The job was difficult and the hours grueling. Sometimes, when there were supplier issues, we worked as many as 30 consecutive days.

That's where I developed my weird NOT sleeping habits. We would get off work at 2:00 or 3:00 AM, go to my house or someone's house and cook dinner, watch a movie, or just hang out till sunrise. We would then go home and sleep till 1:00 or 2:00 PM.

I didn't realize it at the time, but I was learning important lessons about leadership: you can lead without a lot of experience, hanging out together matters, you build trust and respect by getting to know each other outside the workplace. It is a lesson I have not forgotten. And, yes, my weird sleeping habits remain but are becoming more regular with age.

There Is More to My Story

In 2005, Dell began closing our facility and moved their operations to other regions. I was told to lay off half of my employees, people who had been at Dell their entire careers. That was tough. It was hard watching people break down. I didn't have kids; I didn't have many responsibilities. These were people who had families.

Going through that experience was humbling. It taught me a lot. It shaped my ideas about respect and dignity. I learned the importance of non-verbal empathy. Sometimes it's better to listen, that fewer words are better than many, that I can't always make things better, that you show respect by letting people process their own grief. And, because they knew me on a personal level, they understood that I was just doing my job. One colleague that I had to let go said, "This is probably harder on you than it is on me." His words meant a lot.

The lessons that I learned at Dell have helped me, have helped Clint and me, develop the culture we have at SourceDay.

It All Began with a Whiteboard

Clint and I love to tell this story: In 2013, on day one, before we had any idea for a name, we bought a tiny white board for $180. It nearly broke our budget. In our small borrowed office, with our one black Expo Dry Erase Marker, we huddled together, each in a folding chair brought from home. On one side of the white board, we wrote "Culture" and on the other side we wrote "Why". The "why" referred to the mission, the purpose, and the vision of our newly formed company.

Clint and I had both worked at culturally toxic companies: sarcasm was the mode of conversation, backstabbing was the promotion tool, and, in some cases, employees were merely numbers. Animosity permeated and, worst of all, there was nothing challenging about the job. Not surprisingly, people did not want to be there.

We wanted our new company to be different.

The squeaky marker/whiteboard epiphanies that Clint and I brainstormed in 2013 are, to this day, stuck in our brains. They reflect our collective self: transparency, core values, empowerment.

Transparency

From my perspective, I am very open and transparent. I'm guessing most people would say that about themselves. "Hi, I'm honest, open and what you see is what you get." The red flags fly. I'm sure Clint thinks he is transparent. But are we?

Every Tuesday, we meet with our employees to "let it all hang out". Nothing, within the jurisdiction of SourceDay, is off-limits. Usually the conversations are constructive, other times desultory, and, during the pandemic, difficult. Like many companies, we have experienced some pandemic attrition, but I believe our transparency, our open dialogue, has helped employees make the decision to stay on at SourceDay, despite the personal hardships that people have had to endure.

My Transparent Tuesday Comments:
"If you're unhappy, we as leaders are open and here to talk."
"We have resources to help you."
"It's okay if you don't want to be at SourceDay your entire career."
"Maybe there is another role inside of SourceDay."

Transparent Tuesday has also been the catalyst for private conversations. In creating an open, honest work environment, people are more willing to approach Clint and me privately. One employee came to me and said, "I don't like my role anymore." So, we sat down together and talked it out.

We have promoted people to other roles or moved them to other departments within the company because they were open and honest about their goals. If promotion within is not possible, we try to help find a role outside the company. We've helped people do just that. They simply outgrew us. We were either too big or too small. I think companies, too often, put the business ahead of the people.

And I would hope that employees would not shop their salary because they want a raise. I encourage people to come talk to us with their salary concerns. In the last year, I've had three people come to me who were recruited by other companies.

One such employee approached me recently and said, "I've been approached by a recruiter. I love working here. I don't want to leave SourceDay, but this is an opportunity for me to make more money."

I did the research. The compensation concern was justified.

And in that conversation, that tough conversation, I prevented that person from leaving. Salaries matter. A competent employee needs to be paid what she/he is worth.

Core Values

In 2015, we were in a 1000 sq/ft storage closet sublease. Clint and I sat at an old-school lawyer desk facing each other. A makeshift white board was painted on the wall. Clint was primarily responsible for sales and channel partners outreach while I oversaw customer on-boarding, training, support, fundraising, financial models, and demos. That's when we hired our first full-time developer, quality assurance person, and salesperson. The office had eight people. It felt like we were sitting on top of each other.

We needed a bigger space. My neighbor happened to own a 6,000 sq/ft warehouse that was available to lease. It was subdivided into three, 2,000 sq/ft units. The front office had a tiny foyer, a conference room, and a single stall bathroom. The remainder was a 1,600 sq/ft garage with no windows. We signed the lease and SourceDay had a new home. I installed cabinets, countertops, a sink, a disposal, and a drain. Family, friends and our six employees painted the warehouse green and white, our SourceDay colors.

When we moved in, there was only one bathroom: a little awkward but doable. But as we hired more people, it got a little weird, so we rented our neighbor's bathroom for $400 a month. The point is that we were growing rapidly, quickly filling up the 2,000 sq/ft of our "new" warehouse. There was, however, one advantage to our crowded workspace: we were together in one open room.

Here, Clint and I sat next to each other (perhaps we were tired of staring at each other across our desks) with our employees surrounding us. We could hear our sales hunter cold-calling, and we could coach him in real time. "You said this, that was great, but maybe you could have led with an opener that would focus their attention on our value."

The development team, too, was only a few feet away. While on a call, I could swivel my chair and say, "They're asking if we can do this. Can we build it?" They could give me a thumbs up and start to build it before I hung up the phone. It was real time product development. We didn't have the red tape, the bureaucracy, to slow us down. We went fast, making decisions and collaborating in real time.

We worked hard and played hard too. Every now and again, a Nerf bullet would hit me square in the forehead, or an errant football would knock over a lamp, or I would have to duck away from a flying electric RC car, but the craziness was necessary.

We were working together 12 hours a day. The play was a release. The bonding was real. The culture nurturing.

Empowerment

When we were a 10, 12, 20-person company, there was nothing happening at SourceDay that Clint and I didn't know about.

Then we grew to 30 employees, 50, and 100. The company was doing well, but we could no longer oversee everyone and everything. Initially, I struggled with stepping back and trusting our leaders and their teams. I had to learn to take pride in the people we hired, and I had to learn to trust their decisions. And I needed to remember that they're better than me at what they do.

As a result, we have empowered and promoted people in our customer delivery, sales, support, and engineering teams. They make decisions every day that I never know about. We have promoted from within, or hired from without, leaders who are empowered to make decisions for their respective teams. And, because we have established a culture of collaboration, our leaders are not making decisions individually, they are (we are) making decisions as a group.

> PERSPECTIVE: We have recently cut our lease and moved to a beautiful new office building. But our "warehouse" culture remains.

CHAPTER 5
IT'S NOT IMPOSSIBLE

> **LESSSON LEARNED:**
> Embrace challenges.

> "There will be obstacles. There will be doubters. There will be mistakes. But with hard work, there are no limits."
> —Michael Phelps

My degree from Texas A&M is in Industrial Distribution Engineering, specifically supply chain logistics, manufacturing, and distribution. After college, I was hired by Dell to work in manufacturing. It was there that I witnessed first-hand how supply chain issues can bring production to a standstill.

There were many times, for example, when we had to shut down the facility because we didn't have the protective foam end-caps that protect a computer during shipment. Supply chain challenges like this existed everywhere, even at a company the size of Dell.

Clint and I wanted to solve a real-world problem, no matter the size of the organization. We wanted to be the solution for companies who were constantly dealing with roadblocks from their suppliers. Simply put, they were not getting their needed supplies on time. Our goal was to build a solution that drove better supplier collaboration and visibility on the procurement of direct materials.

When Clint and I launched SourceDay in 2015, I was working at a local software company and Clint was at another. A year later, we each left our respective jobs and committed ourselves full-time to SourceDay. There were many obstacles, and we were risking everything.

Obstacle #1: Family Responsibilities

Saying to your wife, "We're going to have to change our lifestyle while I chase this dream" is difficult; doing it can be devastating. Clint went through a divorce, and my marriage was tested.

Our travel plans were put on hold, restaurants were off-limits, and I sold my GMC Sierra pick-up truck. Instead, I borrowed one of my parent's cars.

And there was another "obstacle". I came home one night after work and Autumn met me at the door. I could tell she had been crying. Her hands were shaking as she raised the unmistakable plastic stick. It was pink. I smiled. We hugged. Internally, I was terrified. You're never ready for a child, even if you already have two. "We'll figure it out," I said.

Obstacle #2: Finances

We maxed out our credit cards, borrowed money and I cleaned out my 401k so I could keep our house and make sure Autumn had a vehicle large enough for three kids.

Obstacle #3: Improving Supply Chain Performance

My mom went to school later in life to become a teacher. She graduated first in her class at the University of Texas. She is organized, intelligent, and stubborn. I am too. I get my work ethic from both of my parents, but my stubbornness from Mom. She has that no-quit, anything-is-possible entrepreneurial spirit. She is not afraid to take on the more uncommon and "impossible" projects.

Clint and I prescribe to the mentality of "not impossible." That "not impossible" mindset has helped us realize that what we accomplished at SourceDay, as an early-stage company, was impossible, or, at the very least, improbable. We created a large network of suppliers for direct materials, enabling collaboration and driving more just-in-time manufacturing. We improved supply chain performance.

It was not easy. The marketplace and the network that we built had been tried several times in the late 90's by companies that don't exist anymore. We read those case studies, and we met some of those early founders. "You're crazy. It can't be done," they said. Their words only motivated us more. And with the technology available in 2013, with Cloud and SaaS software platforms becoming the norm, we knew that we could make it happen.

We were also told, "It's a fool's errand to try and build a two-sided network where you have to get suppliers to voluntarily use the platform." But it was not a fool's errand. Initially, we got a lot of "No's" or "We don't even have a computer" or "We don't have an email address," but we persevered.

How did we do it? When we signed up a new customer, Clint and I trained every one of their suppliers in person or virtually, one at a time, to get them on the platform. We even traveled to China once to train a supplier. It was tedious but necessary work.

Obstacle #4: Fundraising

Growing up, I watched my dad forgo higher salaries in favor of more equity at start-up companies because he believed in the business and the founder. He was able to build a successful career by being the higher risk taking CFO. As a start-up, you're going to take the experienced person that is willing to take less money and more risk on the stock upside. He did that his entire career.

I watched him build companies, raise money, and go on several IPO (initial public offering) roadshows. He took two companies public and sold four or five more. When I was starting my first company, RightGift, he was the CFO of RetailMeNot. I get my passion for entrepreneurship from my dad.

Early on, Clint and I raised money from friends and family, but we quickly tapped that out. My father, too, contributed a bit of money, but I was unwilling to ask him for more. I was happy just to have his moral support and professional experience.

So, we moved beyond friends and family to venture investors. A hundred times they said, "No." They were hesitant because we had no customers and no market, and, to borrow a line from *Star Trek*, because we were boldly going into a new category where no man or woman had gone before.

But we persisted. Finding investors requires networking, and Clint and I used our network. It's knowing somebody who trusts you, who will vouch for you. Our first venture money was from Chris Shonk at ATX Ventures. We met him at a restaurant in downtown Austin. Armed with only an idea, a piece of the platform, a pitch deck, and, most importantly, our passionate commitment to make it happen, we made our pitch. Chris said yes and wrote us a check for nearly a half-million dollars. That money enabled us to continue building the business.

Early on, with investors like Chris, we were looking for mentorship and monetary support. However, as our company scaled up, value "beyond just dollars" became a priority. We were careful to partner with investors/firms that were helpful in recruiting talent, scaling operations, building realistic but aggressive growth plans, and fostering strategic partners.

Our objective was to have a variety of board members who engage in discussions that challenge the business plan, operations, growth targets, spending and, ultimately, what an exit may look like.

Today, we have over a dozen investors who believe in our team, our company, and our commitment to drive better supplier/manufacturer collaboration. We are grateful for their strategic and financial support.

PERSPECTIVE: Raising money at that time, especially pre-revenue money, was improbable on an idea alone. But it was not impossible.

CHAPTER 6
UNSUNG HEROES

> **LESSSON LEARNED:**
> Buyers need tools.

> "A hero is an ordinary individual who finds the strength to persevere and endure in spite of an overwhelming obstacle."
> —Christopher Reeve

I've always maintained that the buyers within organizations are the unsung heroes of any physical product company. I tell this to every analyst, customer, and investor that I know.

Meet Average Jane: She is a buyer for an average manufacturer. She has been given no tools, no systems, no processes. She is told, "Here are thousands of lines of POs and parts that you need to process on-time and in-full. And, if you miss even one of them, it is your fault."

Armed with guile, guts, and determination, Average Jane is expected to purchase parts and finished goods to keep her company's production up and running. But when she sends a PO to her average supplier, there is usually no PO acknowledgement and, many times, the parts show up late, missing, or worse, not at all.

And when there is collaboration via email, Excel, or phone, the process is so slow that, once again, the parts show up late. An average conversation might begin like this:

Supplier: "Here are some changes that I need to propose because we can't meet your dates, your quantities, or your price point."

Jane: "Ugh."

Disruption

"Disruption" became an important buzz word for startup founders in the early 2000's. They wanted to be "disrupters". To me, disruption means taking an existing workflow process and improving it. In our little vignette above, Average Jane needs some serious disrupting.

When Clint and I built our platform, our goal was to help buyers like Jane be more strategic and efficient. We were chasing an elusive problem; buyers were living in Excel, which are error-prone, one-person, static documents that are not collaboration friendly. We wanted to give the unsung heroes a platform to help them better serve their businesses and their customers.

Sellers, marketers, and engineers have tools like CRMs (customer relationship management) and PLMs (product lifestyle management) to help them be more efficient and more effective.

But in the procurement world, buyers of direct materials have nothing. They are thrown to the proverbial wolves and told, "Figure it out and make it happen".

So, we thought, why shouldn't buyers have tools too?

Our Own Unsung Hero

In October of 2016, Clint and I created our first SourceDay YouTube video. It cost us $2,000 to produce. We had no money, so we charged it to a credit card. It was the best $2,000 we ever spent.

As fate would have it, at the same time, a Fortune 50 technology and manufacturing company had a project to digitize the procurement of their global service parts. They were looking for a solution to do exactly what we do: remove the manual process, digitize, and increase communication and collaboration between the supplier and the ERP (enterprise resource planning). We received an inbound from an employee at this company who saw our video.

Backstory: In March of every year, Clint and I attend he SUN (Syteline User Network) Conference. We show our demo and promote our SourceDay product on stage. We usually return to Austin with renewed enthusiasm and dozens of leads.

Our dilemma: This Fortune 50 technology manufacturer wanted us on site at their home office in Round Rock the very same week we were attending The SUN conference in Nashville. The prospect's executives were coming in from all over the world and wanted to see our SourceDay demo.

Did we attend the conference or drive to Round Rock to meet with their executives?

We went to the conference. Our reasoning? Clint and I are the face of SourceDay. We were building the business together. There were going to be over 100 customers at SUN. I am always the optimist. I believe we can accomplish anything, but I didn't think we would land a whale at this stage in our journey. I told Clint, "This is one of the biggest companies in the world. There is no way. They must be confused."

So, we sent Colby Young, our junior sales rep.

I'll never forget the phone call. "I knocked it out of the park. They want to continue to talk. They want to meet with us further," said Colby.

After vetting us thoroughly, Keith Wolf, an executive from the prospect company called us. "We need to talk. Let's get some beers together." We met at a local pub. We ordered our beers. I pulled out my credit card, but Keith stopped me. "I want to pay for these beers because I want you to remember this. I'm going to take a chance on you guys and your start-up. We're going to award you the business." Within a month, we had a signed agreement. We had landed a whale. They are still one of our largest clients.

Update

I saw Keith last week at a golf tournament. He reminded me of our meeting at the Austin pub in 2016. And he added this insight: "Your sales rep's first demo stalled our entire buying process with your competitors. We ended up going down a path with you all because your SourceDay product spoke for itself, and your sales guy delivered it."

PART 1: TOM KIELEY'S STORIES

Colby was our unsung hero. Now we sing his praises. (Read more about Colby in Chapter 8)

> **PERSPECTIVE:** Building a business can be all consuming. But, for me, it's important to take the time to recognize and celebrate the unsung heroes, whether they be our customers that we serve or the colleagues I work with. It helps me to remember the "why" of it all.

CHAPTER 7
THE BEST LAID PLANS

> **LESSSON LEARNED:**
> Some mistakes are fortuitous, some not so much.

> "If you're not making mistakes, then you're not doing anything. I'm positive that a doer makes mistakes."
> —John Wooden

Mistake #1

I come from a woodworking family. While growing up, my father taught me how to make desks, cabinets, tables, beds, and the like. My brother-in-law Mike is a professional furniture maker.

I had just finished building my fiancé a desk for her birthday and was in the process of building the accompanying chair. Surrounded by a jointer, planer, table saw, drill press and more in my dad's pristine woodshop in our oversized garage, I was cutting the leg on the router table.

It was 8:00 PM. I had worked all day at the office and my eyes were at half-mast, and I had to stifle the occasional yawn. As I was guiding the curved chair leg through the router, the router caught an edge. In an instant, my hand was pulled between the fence and the bit.

I screamed. Blood was everywhere.

Fortunately, my family was home. They sprinted into the garage. They rushed me to the kitchen, opened the faucet slightly and gently placed my hand underneath. When the blood cleared, we saw that my middle finger was hanging, connected only by a piece of skin, and my ring finger was spaghetti.

My parents drove me to the hospital. They called my fiancé and my best friend on the way. I sat in the back with my hand wrapped in a towel not feeling much pain. I must have been in shock.

When we arrived, I was able to walk into the hospital. A nurse looked into my eyes. "He's about to pass out," he said. They wheelchaired me to patient portal #1.

Fortunately, one of Austin's best plastic surgeons was on staff at Seton's Medical Center and on-call that evening. The diagnosis was quick. Part of my knuckle was gone. But the biggest concern was the tendons. They had receded. The doctor had to pull the tendon back down into my hand and reconstruct it.

The surgery was a success and almost pain free. The only painful part was the lidocaine injections that numbed my fingers.

After physical therapy (I had to wear a custom made rubber band sling on my middle finger every day for six months), I can now bend my finger almost completely forward. I am forever grateful to the doctor and his staff.

PERSPECTIVE: I learned two things on that fateful router ruined night. That I shouldn't use a router when I'm tired, and that I don't have quit in me. As soon as I could, I got back into the wood shop and continued to make beds, tables, and desks. The falling off the proverbial horse maxim is true for me. Well sort of. I have yet to make another chair.

Mistake #2

"Most entrepreneurs will admit luck plays a part in success."
—Richard Branson

In 2013, we hired Matt Suttles as a program developer. He helped build our platform from the ground up. He became The Godfather's right-hand man. Matt rarely made mistakes. We're grateful he made this one. It changed the way we do our business with our customers and their suppliers.

What was his mistake?

We had asked each of our customers (manufacturers) to create for us a list of suppliers who they thought might benefit from our software; suppliers who would need little or no training. Our customers were careful to exclude any supplier who might be hesitant to try something new, something out of their comfort zone. As per usual, our plan was to contact those hesitant suppliers separately, offering them training and support to get them on board.

Matt and Mehedi had just completed writing the platform for the above software, but they made a mistake on a piece of the code. As a result, instead of sending an invitation to the carefully selected list of computer savvy suppliers, the invitation to join SourceDay was sent to ALL our customer's suppliers. It appeared that we had purposely ignored their lists and were pushing our SourceDay software on everyone.

Unknowingly, we had "accidentally" spammed over five-thousand suppliers, inviting them to use software they knew nothing about. Our customers were angry. They felt betrayed. "Why did we take the time to create the list if you were going to ignore it? Why are you pushing your product on all our suppliers?" they asked.

I have a motto that I tell our team members, "When writing code or doing anything new, if you're not breaking something, then you're not innovating fast enough; you're not creating something new." Fortunately, Matt had listened.

Why was his mistake fortuitous?

We called an impromptu damage control meeting to discuss and brainstorm fixes to the above disaster. After the meeting, with heads down and feet shuffling, Matt and his team of program engineers dragged their heavy hearts and bruised egos back to their workstations. Humility filled the air.

Soon, however, the mood in the office began to change. As our programmers were looking at their computer screens, their body language transformed. At first there were disbelieving stares, then leaning in, then gaping mouths, and, finally, contented smiles. Our office became a cacophony of joy. "Suppliers are accepting our invitations. They are using the software that we 'accidently' sent them," they said. Over a hundred suppliers, including some that were not on the approved lists, had signed on without any prompting, without any training.

PART 1: TOM KIELEY'S STORIES

Our heads exploded. An aha moment ensued: Suppliers are smart. They will realize the benefits of using our software. Why are we pushing and pulling suppliers to join the platform? Why are we force feeding them?

As a result, our new and improved on-boarding process was born. Our old sales pitches were abandoned. Now we send a friendly email to suppliers with a list of benefits and assume the close. They use the platform because it's advantageous for them. And, if a supplier is hesitant, we say, "You need to join SourceDay. This is how you're going to do business with your customer. It's free and it's to your advantage."

Of course, we don't send invitations to all the suppliers. We control it. We still train about 40% of them when they request it, but, thanks to Matt's mistake, signing on suppliers (the core to our business) is more manageable, and we can tailor our training to the ones that really need our assistance. A fortuitous mistake indeed.

PERSPECTIVE: There is a connection between launching a start-up and woodworking. With both, you're starting from scratch and creating something that has never been built. With both, you need the best raw materials and the tools to create a quality product. And having competent, caring people around you can make all the difference, especially when you slice off a finger, metaphorically or otherwise.

NOTE: Matt Suttles stayed at the company for four years and moved on to a new role at another company, but he is still a good friend.

CHAPTER 8
EARLY-STAGE PEOPLE

> **LESSSONS LEARNED:**
>
> 1. In the early stage of a start-up, hire generalists.
>
> 2. Many early-stage generalists become successful late-stage A-players.

> "He who is not courageous enough to take risks, will accomplish nothing in life."
> —Muhammed Ali

According to the December 2020 Forbes.com article 10 Critical Qualities Every Startup Hire Should Have, "Working for a startup is vastly different than working for an established company. Established companies have steady processes and defined operations, while startups often wade through a constant stream of pivots and unknowns."

To support their assertion, Forbes asked 10 members of the Young Entrepreneur Council the traits they deemed essential for startup employees. Here is their list:

1. The ability to be fearless through failure
2. A passion for your mission
3. A proactive attitude
4. A willingness to take risks
5. A preference for unstructured systems
6. Relentlessness
7. Courage
8. Self-motivation
9. The ability to prioritize company goals over personal goals
10. Belief in the company's vision

Early-Stage Generalists

Phillip Pavelka

In 2016, four years before the publication of the above Forbes article, we hired Phillip Pavelka. He had previously worked under Clint's supervision at a manufacturing firm in Austin. Clint didn't have the above Young Entrepreneur Council list to assist him, but, because they had worked side by side, he believed that Phillip would be perfect for our startup.

At the time of Phillip's hire, we had two customers and a lot of free time. We were "working" out of the closet space that we had sublet from Austin Rare Coins. When Phillip arrived at "the closet" on his first day, Clint and I were leaning forward in our leather swivel chairs, joy sticks in hands, racing cars on our XBox.

PART 1: TOM KIELEY'S STORIES

When we looked up from our competitive video game, Phillip was standing behind us. We had no idea how long he had been there. "I quit my job and risked my family's well-being for this? I think I just made the biggest mistake of my life," he said.

It wasn't.

Despite the inauspicious beginning, Phillip was indeed a perfect fit for us. Initially, he helped Clint with on-boarding, but soon, as our client number increased and our XBox time decreased, he became our right-hand man. He took over the on-boarding of our suppliers and became our demo person, presenting over 1,200 product demos to customers and prospects.

Taking over this role was essential because a company looks small and insignificant if the co-founder/CEO is giving demos to the prospects. He observed my demo style and cadence, tweaked it, and successfully made it his own. Phillip is still with the company. He is now a Sales Director in our Infor Syteline/CSI ecosystem.

Colby Young

Our first sales hire was Colby Young who, ironically, didn't have much sales experience. What he did have was a master's degree in business, an analytical mind, and a relentless hunger to learn every role in our company. He had his hands in marketing, email, demos, and content. Colby's goal was to, someday, create his own start-up.

Fortunately for us, Colby is still part of our team. He is the VP of our NetSuite Business Unit. He has a team of sellers and a channel manager that report to him. (Read more of Colby's story in Chapter 6)

Nancy Kuemmerle

Nancy was a contractor that we hired early on. She is a good example of an early-stage generalist. She was responsible for hiring, firing, benefits, accounting, finance, and payroll. She made sure people got paid on time, received their proper benefits, and were in a safe environment.

Today, Nancy's role is more specific, but her dedication to our SourceDay vision remains.

She is our HR director officer manager. When Covid hit, she became part counselor, helping employees through challenging times, whether work related or not.

Colby, Nancy and Phillip still have the Young Entrepreneur Council traits that helped them be successful in SourceDay's early stage. They have transitioned successfully into a more late-stage role because they are proactive, relentless, and have a passion for our SourceDay mission. Their early-stage experience gave them the insight and expertise to be successful in a more specific late-stage role.

Kyle Kothe

Kyle was a minority co-founder of BIDsmash (which later became SourceDay). He helped me design and develop the user interface for my initial company RightGift. Kyle then helped us do the same with BIDsmash/SourceDay by creating our website and application UI (user interface).

Kyle is now the CEO and co-founder of RightGift. He relaunched the business in 2018 and has been leading it ever since.

PART 1: TOM KIELEY'S STORIES

PERSPECTIVE: When launching a start-up, hire generalists who can handle many roles, and outsource the others. For example, we had a marketing consultant who helped us set up email campaigns and build our website. We outsourced all our HR, payroll, accounting, benefits, state and federal tax filings, and website design.

CHAPTER 9
THE SOLIDARITY OF SUCCESS

> **LESSSON LEARNED:**
> There is more to success than money.

> "Strive not to be a success, but rather to be of value."
> —Albert Einstein

When my sister Erin found my 13-year-old body gasping for air in the middle of the night, she didn't panic. She called 911. I owe her my life.

Because of my chronic childhood asthma, I was hospitalized several times while growing up.

But asthma didn't keep me from athletics. I loved to compete, and perhaps because of the asthma incident above, I didn't want to compete alone. I felt I needed to be part of a team. I tried every sport: soccer, baseball, basketball, roller hockey, and football. Each with limited success.

During one of my checkups, when my doctor said, "You should really think about swimming because swimming exercises your lungs; your lungs are just a muscle. You're changing your breathing patterns and you're holding your breath at different intervals," I listened. When he reminded me that swimming was a team sport, I acted. I dropped all the other sports and joined the Texas Gold swim team. I loved it.

Two years later, I was part of the first ever swim team at Anderson High School. And that team ended up winning State the year after I graduated. I'm still friends with all those guys.

Being part of my middle school and high school swim teams taught me about dedication and teamwork, lessons I carry with me today.

Dedication and Teamwork

"Success: the achieving of the results wanted or hoped for."
—Cambridge Dictionary

To me, success is giving each team member an opportunity to build his/her career. My hope is that my people, my colleagues, grow their careers inside SourceDay. And, as painful as it is to lose good people, I take pride in seeing them get bigger roles outside of SourceDay.

Success is also about making money. Whether it be team members, investors, stakeholders, or me, on some level monetary success matters. But it's only part of the equation. If we hire people who are only chasing monetary gains, they're going to fail because they are going to make short term decisions to achieve short term success. It starts with hiring people who love the challenge of a start-up and who see an opportunity to improve the procurement world.

If people are at the office every day because they love the customer, love the disruption we are creating, love the outcome we are building, and, yes, love the monetary success, they will succeed long-term.

Full Disclosure: Clint and I could have sold the business in the last round of funding. Instead of worrying about raising money, we could have made a healthy profit and walked away. But would we have achieved success? Short term: yes. Long term: no.

One of my long-term goals is for the people who have invested their time, who have made personal sacrifices, and who have dedicated years of their careers to our SourceDay vision to make a significant return and experience they can take onto their next ventures. We are all working to build SourceDay from the ground up. It is not easy. To my earlier point, if we would have exited early, it would be unfinished business, the ultimate failure.

PERSPECTIVE: Whether it's on a swim team or in a start-up business, success is dedication to what you do, enjoying who you are working (or swimming) with, and making a difference in the world. We had that at Texas Gold and at Anderson High School, and we have that at SourceDay.

NOTE: Our initial slogan iteration for SourceDay was #BtheB. It stood for Be the Billion. As a company that depended on investors, we needed to set lofty goals. A billion dollars is a nice target, but, ultimately, it was one-dimensional. Our slogan, our mantra, is still #BtheB, but now it encompasses a more holistic definition of success. #BtheB stands for Be the Best.

CHAPTER 10
TRANSCENDING THE WORKPLACE (GIVING BACK)

> **LESSSON LEARNED:**
> Culture and community are forever linked.

> "Always build communities inside and outside of work. A place is much stronger when people are connected."
> —Eric Schmidt, The Trillion Dollar Coach

When I was growing up, my parents instilled in me the importance of giving back to the community. My father and I, for example, did volunteer construction work for Habitat for Humanity. We helped build houses around Austin.

Clint's parents also believed in community service. So, when we launched SourceDay, we knew it was our responsibility, even at a small company like ours, to use the power of our company, the power of our SourceDay workforce, to give back. It was in our DNA. We understood, too, that we were fortunate to have the opportunity to start a company. So, we wanted to create similar opportunities for students in the Austin community.

Clint and I created a committee called SourceDay Cares. It is a small group of leaders from different departments. The committee meets every other Friday. Clint and I are the executive sponsors. We approve budget items, but the community service outreach is the responsibility of the committee.

Our purpose? We want to improve our SourceDay community by giving back to the Austin community (and beyond).

Pre-Covid: The Central Texas Food Bank

SourceDay takes meal packaging very seriously. Our record is twelve-thousand meals packaged and shipped out in one day. Pre-Covid, our teams would arrive at The Central Texas Food Bank, spend the morning packaging meals and then, depending on when we finished, have lunch or dinner together. We did that once every quarter. The boxes we put together were shipped to homeless shelters and the like.

Working at the food bank was a perfect fit for us because of our supply chain and manufacturing expertise. "How can we make this more efficient?" "How can we beat our numbers each quarter?" "Is the lead process more efficient than the staggered individual process?" We would "game it" because we love competition.

Brady's Bridge

We also support a non-profit organization called Brady's Bridge. Tabitha Fry is the founder and CEO. Her organization supports the parents of children with special needs by providing child care. Typically, one parent must quit his or her job to take care of their child, putting a financial burden on the family.

Brady's Bridge makes it possible for both parents to work. Parents have peace of mind knowing that their child is in a state-of-the-art child care facility, staffed by caring, understanding professionals. The cost is subsidized so families are not burdened with the high fees that might otherwise exist.

Tabitha recently opened her first special needs, child care facility and plans to create similar non-profit franchises around the country.

So, when she reaches out to us, we are honored to help. We band together as a company and get the job done. For example, every holiday season Tabitha delivers hundreds of Christmas trees and gifts to children in hospitals around the city. We do our small part with the packaging and delivery.

We also help by staffing the Brady Bridge 5K Fun Run. All of us at SourceDay (except those staffing the event) and our families dress up in our green SourceDay gear and participate in the fun run. The proceeds go to facility costs, teacher salaries, special needs equipment, and more.

Scholarships and Internships

Huston-Tillotson is an historically black university. It was established in 1875 and is Austin's oldest. After the George Floyd killing in May of 2020, our SourceDay Cares team met. Our goal was to impact real change: to do something that would make a lasting difference. So, we created a scholarship fund at Huston-Tillotson.

The fund grants two minority students five-thousand dollars each. These students are typically one semester shy of graduation who need the extra funding to graduate.

We have also expanded our internship program to include more students from Huston-Tillotson. The internship programs help students get real world, business, corporate office environment experience. The students get class credit and receive a salary as part of their internship program.

We believe it is our responsibility to support equality (equal opportunity) for every race and background.

Random Things

We do random things too: For example, we have employees in Ukraine. So, when Russia invaded Ukraine, we put together a dollar-matched contribution. We sent $5,000 to two Ukraine specific charities that our CMO Sarah Scudder helped us choose.

When tragedies happen: a tornado, a hurricane, or a social issue that needs attention, we feel it is our obligation to help the cause.

PERSPECTIVE: When we reach out to the community, we gain personally because we are helping others. It simply feels right and good to impact the world in a positive way. And there is an added advantage: we love coming to work because we are part of something bigger than ourselves.

CHAPTER 11
THE TALE OF TWO PITCHES

> **LESSSON LEARNED:**
> To investors, the person matters most.

> "Winning comes from a willingness to fail."
> —Tim Draper

The Worst of Pitches

Backstory: In 2009, when I was attempting to launch my first start-up, RightGift, I met Morgan Flager. At the time, he worked at Silverton Partners, one of the most successful investment firms in Texas. I'd taken RightGift to a point where I thought I could raise some much-needed money. Through my networking connections, I was able to schedule my first ever startup pitch in front of Morgan and his colleagues at Silverton.

Backstory to my backstory: I'm bad at rehearsing, especially speeches and start-up pitches. It feels artificial to pitch to someone who is only there for moral support. If I know the content, then my charm and good looks will take care of the rest. Who needs to practice? Teachers loved me in middle school and high school. "Tom, you're a natural," they told me.

The meeting with Silverton was in a hundred-year-old house in downtown Austin, their home base. As I walked up the terracotta steps, I was nervous. When you've mortgaged your future and your financial well-being on a start-up, the stakes are a bit higher than getting a good grade on your "Endangered Whale" speech in 8th grade.

At the time I was 27 years old. I didn't know much about anything, and, worse yet, I didn't know that I didn't know anything about anything (I'll give you a moment to process that.)

My hand quivered as I reached out to grab the antique glass knob that might be opening the door to my entrepreneurial future. I entered the restored mansion lobby and waited to be called into the small office to pitch my RightGift idea. To paraphrase Bob Seger, "Sweat poured out my body, like the music that I played." Only I wouldn't be playing music. I would be playing my future, my family's future.

I thought I knew the content.

I didn't.

In the politest voices they could muster, the Silverton investors tore me apart, telling me the truth about where my RightGift business model was flawed:

"You need to put more thought into how RightGift is going to grow and be profitable."

"You have almost no plan to target and acquire users."

PART 1: TOM KIELEY'S STORIES

"You have no clue about how much user acquisition will cost, and, without that insight, it will be impossible to invest because there is no path to understanding profitability."

"You need to have more data on user acquisition." (a common problem for consumer apps)

"You need to know more about what it takes to successfully run a company through the many phases of growth."

They were essentially telling me that I didn't know anything about anything.

As I descended the steps outside the 100-year-old converted mansion that was the Silverton office building, the rhythmic sound of my wing-tipped footfalls reverberated the baked earth drumbeat of failure.

But I did not give up. Quitting is not in my genetic makeup. Instead, I learned from my first pitch mistakes. I learned that I needed a comprehensive business plan, and, more specifically, I needed to "know my numbers," including an understanding of client acquisition.

There were other lessons learned: For example, I needed to have a narrow "target" synergistic market (the whole is greater than the sum of its parts) to prove that I could "rinse and repeat" the model/cost process.

But, most importantly, I learned that I needed to give the investors a reason to believe in me.

PERSPECTIVE: When investors put "first money" into a company, they're investing in the person. Of course, the idea and the market matter, but the essential question is, "Can the founder take the idea to the next level?" If a more prepared, more knowledgeable person had presented RightGift to Silverton Partners, they might have funded the venture, even if the idea was a little flawed. I have never forgotten that realization.

The Best of Pitches

Turn the Page to 2016: Clint and I were raising first round money for SourceDay, our new company. We pitched to Chris Shonk at ATX Ventures. Because I had learned from my previous RightGift pitch fiasco, and because Clint demanded it, we were successful. Much of our preparation time was spent problem solving how to target our addressable market (TAM) users. (Our model at SourceDay is still an outbound and partner model.)

As a result, ATX became our first major investor.

It Gets Better

A year and several hundred hours of spreadsheets and slide creations later, when we were in the Series Seed round, I reached out again to Morgan Flager at Silverton Partners. He agreed to a meeting. Clint and I climbed the terracotta steps, the second time for me, confidently turned the glass, antique doorknob and entered the restored hundred-year-old mansion/office building. We made our pitch to Morgan and his colleagues. Shortly after, Morgan wrote us a term sheet.

And Better

The very next day, we received a competitive term sheet from Tim Draper at West Coast VC. Here we were, two neophytes who had never negotiated a term sheet, simultaneously navigating two.

We thought, perhaps we could negotiate a deal where both parties agree on the terms. So, I brought them together. Tim Draper led the round. He set the valuation of SourceDay based on the term sheet, and Silverton Partners agreed to fund an equal dollar amount. As a result, they came into that round as equal investors. And we received a much needed 3.5 million dollars.

Having Silverton, which was the top investment firm in Texas and arguably one of the best in the country, and Tim Draper, one of the biggest names in venture capital, co-leading a round for our little company in Austin, Texas was a confirmation. We knew, from that moment, that SourceDay would be a success. So did Tim Draper and Morgan Flager. They believed in us.

> NOTE: Morgan joined our board in June of 2017 and has been a partner and friend of the business ever since. He helps us hire executives, get through strategic times, navigate partnerships, and make financial decisions.

> PERSPECTIVE: Having people the caliber of Morgan and Silverton on the board at an early stage matters.

DUG UP FROM MY OLD NOTES: A TIMELINE OF RANDOM THOUGHTS AND NOT-SO-RANDOM PEOPLE

May 2014—Clint McRee: We realize that we must pivot from our original model. Clint and I are going through many months of back and forth. Should we shut down the business or continue on? Emotions are high with debt and family challenges due to all the time we are spending on the business. Following the advice from other founders, we charge forward.

March 2015—Jack Daniels: The initial SUN (SyteLine User Conference), our first big event. We fly to Nashville. Clint has the idea to give away airport-sized bottles of Jack Daniel's to attract people to our booth. Our credit cards are declined attempting to buy hundreds of bottles, no doubt because we are in another state at a small liquor store spending money we don't have. The bottles are a HUGE hit. People drop by our booth, chat about supply chain procurement, and sneak away with a handful of bottles.

August 2015—Melissa and Kevin Wolter: Autumn and I move into our new home and become friends with our new neighbors, the Wolters. Kevin is intrigued with investing in a startup and, as we become closer friends, he asks to invest in our Family and

Friends Round. I am hesitant at first knowing how these things can ruin relationships. Kevin convinces me that he understands the risks, but he still wants to be a part of the journey. He and Melissa invest in SourceDay.

PERSPECTIVE: I do not ever recommend mixing business with personal, but we are fortunate because we remain great friends today.

November 2016—Paul Bell: I meet Paul Bell at an ATX Ventures Investor event. I recognize Paul from my years at Dell when Paul was President. I approach him for a meeting, hoping he will become my mentor.

July 2017—Paul becomes a member of our Board of Advisors.

February 2018—Paul becomes a strategic addition to our Board of Directors as an Independent Board seat.

PERSPECTIVE: It's critical to build relationships with executives and leaders that have done it before.

Jan 2019—Kirk Dando: By introduction from Morgan Flager at Silverton Partners, I hire Kirk Dando as my executive coach. Kirk helps me and the leadership team build a cadence of accountability and alignment. With his coaching and strategy sessions, we put in several strategies that help us scale our business and people through each phase of growth. Kirk helps me understand that every organization needs different people, systems, and processes through scale and that recognizing those changes early is critical to velocity.

PERSPECTIVE: Being a young-ish, first-time CEO, the imposter syndrome is real. I have my family, advisors, and mentors but, as CEO, I often find myself in situations where I really need an experienced coach to share and work through the most confidential decisions and strategies.

October 2019—Peter Feldman: We hire Peter as CTO. He is the comedian of the group, always keeping even the most difficult times light. Peter owns all things: product, quality engineering, engineering, customer implementations, and security. Peter comes from several successful startups and is able to carry multiple leadership positions for us while we build out the organization.

July 2019—I realize I'm terrible at managing my time and calendar. I need to let go of things and trust my team. Burnout is very real and, if I'm not taking time for myself and my family, my team will suffer. Exercising with my neighbors three or four days a week to start my day becomes a necessary routine to keep my sanity.

August 2019—I begin to use a calendar

September 2019—Jim Hilbert: We have been without a sales leader. After several months of searching, we hire Jim Hilbert. Jim brings a rich background in executive leadership, supply chain experience, and successful startup exits for this critically strategic role. He is a true servant leader. I continue to learn from his leadership.

March 2020—We have just moved into our new space that was 7x the size and cost of our previous space. COVID becomes a thing that nobody understands. As if starting a company and disrupting an industry weren't hard enough, now we must manage through an unprecedented pandemic.

We have a term sheet to close our Series B in hand, we're running out of money, and the U.S. is completely shut down. The close of our Series B is delayed. I'm in full panic mode. This is beyond anything I thought I would ever experience.

March 16, 2020—The leadership team and I hold an emergency meeting and agree that we have to close the office. For the first time in our existence, we lose our office culture and the connectivity that fuels us through the challenges all startups face.

April 2020—Joanna Arras: Through several calls and partnering with our investors, we successfully close our Series B on April 1st with Joanna Arras at Baird Capital. I'm incredibly grateful to our team members, investors, and, most importantly, my family who put up with my rollercoaster of emotions.

May 2020—Kendall, Connor, Reese: Because of Covid, I'm working from home. It dawns on me that I have missed much of my children's childhood. The countless nights and weekends building SourceDay have taken their toll. But I find solace knowing that, as we quarantine, I can spend more time with them doing the little things like eating meals together. I often work in our garage so I can watch our kids and the neighbor kids play in the yard. It helps me keep my sanity.

Sept 2020 (Quarter 3)—Coming off one our worst quarters in recent memory, we have our best quarter in the company's history. Demand for supply chain technology is booming. (Note: SourceDay is fortunate to see strong growth as we continue to focus on our industry and narrow our audience to organizations that are growing in these difficult market conditions.)

October 2021—Sarah Scudder: We hire Sarah as our CMO. She suggests that Clint and I write a book to tell our SourceDay story.

December 2021—Maureen Myrick retires. We are thankful that we were able to talk our long-time family friend out of early retirement in January of 2018. We hired Maureen because we needed an expert to bring us process improvement for customer onboarding, support, and growth. Before retiring, Maureen built and led our Customer Success and Support functions. She hired amazing team members that are still a part of SourceDay. Enjoy your retirement, Mo.

February 2022—Sean Jacobsohn: We sign our Series C Team term sheet with Sean Jacobsohn of Northwest Partners for $31.5 million after several emergency board meetings and legal calls on Christmas Eve. This is a surreal moment of growth and accomplishment as we can now invest in our people, hiring, and driving more customer value.

March 2022—We start writing the book.

> "Passion Is Born When Your Heart Gets Carried Away With A Purpose Greater Than Yourself."
>
> —ROY SPENCE

PART 2

CLINT MCREE
COO & CO-FOUNDER

CLINT'S DEDICATION:

To my parents, thanks for being my rock. To my sons, Lake and Heath, watching you grow up and chase your dreams, push through adversity, overcome obstacles, and achieve success has been one of my life's greatest joys. This book is dedicated to you all. Family first, Always!

P.S. To Lake and Heath, MJ is the G.O.A.T!

CHAPTER 1
MY RESTLESS ENTREPRENEURIAL MIND

> **LESSSON LEARNED:**
> Suppliers need to be connected to stakeholders.

> "Anything can happen if you are willing to put in the work and remain open to the possibility."
> —Michael Jordan

In an attempt to efficiently and effectively capture the essence of supply chain frustration, I wrote the following poem:

When Suppliers Don't Deliver

You can't ship a car with three tires
Nor a TV
If the accompanying remote control is
Missing the little green "power on" button.

Get the parts
Get the people there
Get the tooling right
Turn on the factory

The last thing you want is a missing green button.

People standing around
Equipment that's down
Overtime costs
Second and third shifts to make up
Problems downstream

I knew this then and I know it today. In 2006, I worked for Cypress Technologies in the highest levels of manufacturing: electro-mechanical assembly (EMI) and electronic-manufacturing services (EMS). Everything we built had a cable, a harness, wires, connectors, and circuit boards with resistors and components that were going into our products. We needed thousands of suppliers. It was a complicated business to manage. I oversaw production. My job was to get things built and shipped. It was here that the SourceDay seeds were sown.

Our procurement team was buying parts to service my team. In essence, we were their customer. Every day they logged into our ERP system, ran their reports, and placed purchase orders with suppliers. They also dealt with the difficult task of getting our POs acknowledged. Time was spent expediting materials, chasing late parts, and putting out one fire after another.

PART 2: CLINT McCREE'S STORIES

They were constantly calling and emailing suppliers, and, when frustration reached a crescendo, contacting their managers. They were trying to get updates, trying to push the suppliers for materials, trying to expedite the process so we didn't have down time. I know because I was in constant contact with our procurement team.

Materials were procured in our ERP, but there was no communication system, no visibility, and interaction between buyer and supplier was one-to-one. If a supplier went on a vacation, or got promoted or fired, the relationship and supply line was disrupted. If we were dealing with one or two or five suppliers, it would have been manageable, but we were dealing with thousands of suppliers, purchase orders, and over ten-thousand purchase order lines.

Disruption happened daily and on a big scale. Because our procurement team was crucial for the function of the production line, they were under significant stress, running around with their proverbial heads chopped off. I did not envy them.

Most companies will do whatever it takes to keep their customers. When I was working at the previously mentioned manufacturing company, we supplied mounted spotlights to a customer that was servicing the military. Because our supply chain was such a problem for us, parts were coming in late.

As a result, we were so far behind that we worked overtime, weekends, and multiple shifts to build the spotlights. Anything we built had to be immediately rushed to the airport, loaded on a charter jet, and delivered directly to our customer at our expense. It cost our company tens of thousands of dollars.

Direct Spend

Direct spend is associated with parts and services that go into the products you are building and inventorying. For example, seats, wheels, frames, chains, and handlebars all make up direct spend parts needed for a bike manufacturer to build, sell and ship bikes. And manufacturers need all the parts. No seats equals no sales. And no revenue equals a direct spend problem.

Direct Spend Solutions

I have a restless entrepreneurial mind, and, sometimes, I think it is a curse. Try as I might, I can't stop thinking about the impossible, especially when it comes to business. I see problems that are deemed "impossible" to solve, and I think, *How can it be made possible? How can it be made into a business big enough to matter?*

In 2012, when I transitioned from manufacturing into a new career in software sales, supply chain issues still weighed on my mind. I wondered, *How many of my manufacturing friends are suffering the same supply chain nightmares that I experienced?*

I researched and talked with supply chain and procurement professionals. They told me their horror stories. As I suspected, the disruptions I had experienced in my previous manufacturing job were the norm, not the exception.

And there was no available solution.

That was all the motivation I needed. In the same year that I started my new job in software sales, I wrote the SourceDay executive summary in a Google document and saved it away. Our business model is different today, but my original framework still exists.

PART 2: CLINT McCREE'S STORIES

Fast forward to 2015. As Tom writes in his first chapter, using my original framework, our plan was to work directly with suppliers providing a reverse-auction marketplace for companies to buy products and services.

But our customers and investors were turned off to that. "If you're creating a marketplace, you've got to have a lot of buyers. You need to have even many more suppliers, and building a marketplace is expensive," they said.

So, we pivoted to what we do today: solve complex supply problems for companies.

Our Two Objectives

1. To build a world class software in the cloud that helps companies solve their most complex direct spend and supply chain issues.

In 2016, there weren't any solutions in the industry. Today, there are a few similar to SourceDay, but none are as comprehensive, nor as efficient. Why? Because we integrate to ERP solutions: Infor, Epicor ERP, Oracle NetSuite, SAP, Oracle, etc. To do direct spend right, you have to create a deeply integrated ERP solution.

2. To take ownership of the onboarding of suppliers. We recognize that supply portals fail because of supplier adoption. Simply put, they don't use ERP supplier portals.

Why? Because portals developed by ERP vendors are an afterthought and rarely used. ERP portals create inefficient one-to-one arrangements. Our solution is many-to-many. Meaning that a supplier logging into SourceDay can manage all their customers with one log in. And we take ownership of the on-boarding of the suppliers.

When a customer signs up with us, we have an on-boarding team that interacts with the suppliers, trains them, and sets up their account. And, when a supplier forgets his or her password, (it happens more than you might think) we are there to help, judgment free and with a smile in our hearts.

We also monitor supplier usage and health. If a supplier has not logged in when prompted, our software alerts our team to interact with that supplier: "Hey, are you still there? Did you leave the job? Did something happen?" We leave no chain unlinked.

Empowering Suppliers

In the beginning, we were motivated by our passion to improve buyer/supplier PO collaboration. How did we make it happen? By sticking to our core belief that suppliers are stakeholders and need to be treated as such. No more "beat 'em up on price" and "push on 'em like crazy". It's got to be a partnership.

A hypothetical: If I came into a business where all the internal stakeholders—procurement, sales, leadership, accounts payable, accounts receivable, etc.—use an ERP solution to manage their day-to-day business and said: "Hey, guess what? I've decided you're no longer going to be able to use an ERP solution to run your business. I'm going to take that away. And you're going to run the business using nothing but email and spreadsheets."

The stakeholders would say, "You're crazy. There is no way. We need the ERP to run our business."

PART 2: CLINT MCCREE'S STORIES

My response would be, "That's exactly what you're asking your suppliers to do. You're asking them to be key stakeholders, but you're only spoon feeding them information using nothing but emails and outdated spreadsheets. You've got your suppliers on an island. They're not connected. If you can't run your business without an ERP, how can you expect it of your suppliers? How can they be a great partner if they're disconnected?"

Suppliers are stakeholders and need to be connected to their customers was the core of our original framework and it remains today.

Launching SourceDay

In 2015, armed with real world experience and supply chain knowledge, Tom and I launched SourceDay. We had iterated the software as far along as we could afford. It was time. "Alright Tom, we've got to see if someone is going to pay us to use it," I said.

In fact, we needed to test the market and check a few boxes before we could approach investors. These boxes were:

1. Large addressable market— ✓
2. A working product— ✓
3. Solid co-founders— ✓
4. Product/market fit— ✗
5. Customers— ✗

We had no customers.

My entrepreneurial mind kicked into action. "Let's show it to a few people and see if anyone is willing to pay us to use our software." Pricing really wasn't a concern. We needed customers to be an indicator of our product/market fit.

Fortunately, I had a working list of about 100 potential prospects. We emailed them using, what we later coined, our OG (original gangster) Marketing Email. We hoped for a response in a month or two.

Within 20 minutes we got a hit. "This is exactly what we are looking for. When can I see a demo?" The email was from a stakeholder at a company that makes military communications equipment. So, we got to work. "A demo? A sales deck?" We brainstormed. We researched. We summoned experts and, in a couple of days, we were ready for action.

Because our demo was done remotely at a colleague's house there were a few issues: UPS driver ringing doorbell, dogs barking, dogs really barking when UPS driver rings doorbell, sweating under armpits, airplanes flying lower than humanly possible, and babies crying.

Tom was cool under fire. His tone was confident, his cadence flawless. We had achieved the first major milestone in our journey.

The military communications company never bought Source-Day, but they helped us a lot. They wanted more than just the ability to see PO changes in our solution, they wanted to see the conversation between buyers and suppliers because, in between the data endpoints, is the story of "why."

On our daily platform, we've had thousands of conversations about why data is changing.

At the end of our demonstration we were motivated to ask our own "why" question: "Robert, why did you return our initial cold email?"

PART 2: CLINT McCREE'S STORIES

"We emailed you back because a missing five-dollar part prevented us from shipping two machines last year. We lost a million-dollars in sales," he said.

We hear these stories repeatedly. The frustration is real.

> PERSPECTIVE: My entrepreneurial mind rests a bit easier knowing that we have created software that improves the lives of suppliers and buyers; that there is a greater purpose we are serving.

CHAPTER 2
THINGS THAT MATTER

> **LESSSON LEARNED:**
> SourceDay is about more than just software.

> "Life grows relative to one's investment in it."
> —Marc Benioff

Francine Gets to Go Home (A Children's Story)

Francine works at Universal Electric Corporation (later renamed Starline Holdings, LLC). Francine is a hard worker and cares about doing her job well. Every night, when everyone else goes home at 5 o'clock, Francine sits by herself at her desk for one or two hours and inputs supplier data into her company's ERP system.

Francine is losing precious time with her family. She is sad.

Francine knows that, in the world of supply chain, change is the norm, not the exception: purchase order due dates, prices, and quantities need to be addressed each and every night. She knows that if all the changes don't get entered into their ERP, her company will not have accurate data and will be making bad decisions, and costly mistakes.

That would make Francine even sadder.

Francine is invited to attend a SourceDay software demonstration. Francine doesn't like to be away from her job, but, because she is always looking to improve, she accepts the invitation.

At the demo, Francine learns that when using the SourceDay software, instead of manually inputting purchase order changes from an email, fax, or pdf document, a supplier can directly make changes digitally in a platform.

Francine's interest is piqued. She leans in.

When she hears that, with a click of a button, she can approve data changes and automatically update UEC's ERP system, she asks, "I want to make sure that I understand something. When a supplier makes a change, I review and click the "Accept Changes" button and it updates our ERP?"

"Yes. Whether it's one change or a thousand, one click of a button updates the ERP."

"You do realize that I stay after work every day and input the supplier data manually?"

"Yes, we do."

"So, if we purchase your software, I can be home at 5 o'clock and have dinner with my family?"

"Yes, you can."

Francine is no longer sad. Francine is happy.

The End.

Or Was it the Beginning?

Francine Gets To Go Home is more than just a children's story, it is completely true. Francine was, indeed, able to be home with her family at 5 o'clock because of our software. Empowering her was a lightbulb moment for me. I realized then that we were more than a software solution company because we were offering a different kind of solution. Our hashtag #changelives comes from that story.

When I began my career, before marriage and starting a family, my goals were 100% monetary. I was focused on expensive cars, fast boats, and a nice house.

While I am proud that SourceDay is generating sales and creating value for our investors and partners, I am equally proud that, by solving complex supply chain challenges, we are helping our customers and their suppliers like Francine live better lives.

And I am proud that SourceDay is providing an opportunity for our staff to advance their careers while providing for their families. Those intangibles matter more to me than making money. Ten or fifteen years ago, that would not have been the case.

Why have my priorities changed? One: light bulb moments like Francine's. Two: I went through a divorce in 2016.

In 2015, Tom and I were close to securing our first real funding outside our loyal crowdfunding friends and family. We had a product, four or five customers, a wing, and a prayer. At the same time, my wife told me that she wanted to end our marriage. Here we were, in the early stages of SourceDay, and now I was in the throes of a divorce.

I called Tom.

"Let's shut it down," he said. "Launching a startup is not worth risking your marriage or giving up on your family."

"Tom, I'd do anything to keep my marriage and family intact, but the papers are already filed."

Ambivalence

As I drove away from my Austin suburb home for the final time, I looked in the rear view mirror and watched my manicured lawn, my three-car garage, and my previous life fade into oblivion.

Twenty minutes later, I was fumbling with my keys outside apartment #801 at Falconhead Apartments in Lakeway, Texas. When I finally opened the door and stood in the threshold, I stared into the room. It was a metaphor for my state of mind: empty. For me, entering the apartment was the low point in my life.

All that I had with me was an office chair, clothes, computer, and a Time Warner cable modem. Except for my Jeep, that's all I had to my name. I felt empty sitting on that cold, hard floor in that lonely apartment. I was at an all-time low. Except for the birth of my two boys, it was the realest of emotions I've ever felt. I wanted to ball up in a corner.

But I didn't. Instead, I set up the modem and, while sitting on the linoleum floor, took out my computer and logged into our SourceDay bank account. I couldn't believe what I was seeing. We had received the first round of money from ATX Venture Partners. In a matter of 15 minutes, I had gone from personal despair to professional joy. ATX believed in us. And their investment dollars proved it.

A mom inspired conversation with myself ensued: "Divorce is behind you. You have survived failure and that experience has made you stronger. SourceDay is your new mission now, and you're never going to quit."

From that moment on, I was focused on building SourceDay, being a great business partner with Tom, and, most importantly, raising my two boys.

In Retrospect

I am more patient and less judgmental now, especially with my two sons. I have learned the value of time: that time is finite, that time with my kids is important. I have dedicated my life to making sure that I am there for them. I love just hanging out with Lake and Heath listening to the beats of Drake and other hip hop artists.

Recently, I shared my story of divorce and enlightenment with Chris Shonk, the ATX Venture investor. I wanted Chris and his colleague Brad Bentz to know how appreciative I am that they took a chance on Tom and me. Behind the spreadsheets, the data analytics, and the investor decks, are the stories of people's lives.

When Chris and Brad made the decision to invest in us, they did not know about my divorce and, if they had, I wouldn't have wanted that to impact their decision. But I shared my story with them because I felt they needed to know that their decision to back us helped me through a very dark time in my life and, for that, I'm forever grateful.

One More Story that Matters

Chris Pletcher works at Benchmark Automation, a division of Pro Mach. As a dedicated father, he always attended his daughter's basketball practices. "But there was a problem," he said. "Because I needed to constantly update our ERP system with all the supplier data changes, during her practices I sat on the unforgiving bleacher seats and inputted data into my laptop. Last week my daughter dribbled her basketball over to me and said, 'Dad, you're not watching me practice.'"

"If I had your software, I wouldn't need to bring my laptop to her practices anymore. I could just pay attention to my daughter," he said. Fortunately, Pro Mach purchased our software, and Chris can now focus on more important things.

PERSPECTIVE: For Francine, Chris, and me, what matters is being there for our families. I'm proud that our software, our company, can help people do just that. #changelives

CHAPTER 3
IT DOESN'T WORK

> **LESSSON LEARNED:**
> If suppliers are happy, we are happy.

> "You must always examine what's working, evolve your ideas, and change the way you do things."
> —Marc Benioff

One of the first suppliers to use SourceDay was Barb Sladic. She worked (and still does) at Graybar, an important industrial distributor. Today Graybar is a supplier, supporting almost all of our customers on SourceDay, but it didn't start out that way. I'll never forget Barb's initial SourceDay phone call:

"I can't use this software. It doesn't work."

Not great news when starting a cloud-based start-up.

So, we did what any normal fledgling entrepreneur would

do. We panicked. Then we did what any Texas gentleman would do: we sent her chocolates, and flowers and a card that said, "We are sorry you're struggling. We want to get this right for you, and we would love to learn from you. If you're up for it, are you willing to help us make SourceDay better?"

Barb agreed to help. We are forever grateful: One of our phone conversations follows:

Me: "Tell us what needs to be changed."

Barb: "Not quite everything but a lot. I need to be able to see my customers' priorities and what needs my immediate attention. With your platform, my notes to them are sometimes not visible, or they don't show up at all."

Me: "Thank you."

Barb: "There is more. I need the ability to process purchase order transactions in bulk. Responding to each purchase order line one-by-one is time consuming."

Me: "Thank you."

Barb: "I'm not done. I need the data arranged to my liking. The template needs to reflect Graybar's needs and my customer's needs. What works for one company, doesn't always work for another.

Me: "Thank you."

PART 2: CLINT MCCREE'S STORIES

Barb: "I also need an 'Accept-Reject' button. My customers need immediate feedback and so do I. An "Accept-Reject" would benefit both of us. And I need a more efficient way to manage my open order reports. Right now, I'm having to look at a spreadsheet."

Me: "Thank you."

Based on her feedback, we restructured the SourceDay platform. Now it is much more flexible, and it has the official Barb seal of approval. We are forever indebted because she helped us better understand what suppliers need.

PERSPECTIVE: Even though we don't charge them to use it, suppliers are SourceDay's primary users. What they think and their user experience on our platform matters.

CHAPTER 4
T-SHIRTS AND SPORT COATS

> **LESSSON LEARNED:**
> Persistence matters.

> "Energy and persistence conquer all things."
> —Benjamin Franklin

In the spring of 2017, when the blossoms were beginning to open on the poplar trees, when accelerating growth targets were our motivation, and when limited funds were in our bank account, Tom and I registered to attend a September ERP user conference at the Gaylord Opryland Resort and Convention Center in Nashville, Tennessee.

Our goal was to expand to new markets.

To do that at this conference, our plan was to form a partnership with the ERP vendor. This would keep costs down and, with our goal in mind, allow us to have an exhibit.

Disappointment

I'm not sure why a certain ERP vendor (who shall remain nameless) had it in for us. But, for whatever reason, they blocked our conference partnership. Was it our tacky green t-shirt/sports coat ensemble? or perhaps they thought we were just another start-up company with a good idea and nothing else: no experience, no expertise, no gumption. They might have been right about our attire, but they were wrong about our drive and our expertise. And we had something else they hadn't considered: an unbreakable partnership.

> NOTE: Being blocked by ERP vendors is a theme that would play out for years. It only fueled our motivation.

If at First You Don't Succeed...

So, we tried again. In our second attempt to register for the conference, we shelled out top dollar for full-access conference passes. To our surprise, our tickets were accepted. With new, fully paid tickets in our inbox, we made hotel reservations, booked our flights, and scheduled meetings with partners and prospects.

Because of the time investment, and the ERP vendor partnership issue, we knew going to this conference was risky, and, with our limited budget, there was no room for error. But it was an opportunity we couldn't pass up.

Denied Again

Two days before the event, I received an email from conference headquarters: "Your rooms have been canceled." After some digging and a few profanities, Tom and I learned that the ERP vendor had canceled both of our hotel rooms.

It Gets Worse

Soon after, we received another inbound from the conference. Tom and I leaned into my computer screen and read the email. "Your conference passes have been canceled". Why? because we were not a partner, prospect, or a customer. Tom and I looked up from the screen, turned to each other and exclaimed simultaneously, "Well damn!"

And we had questions:

- "How do we get our money back?"
- "What do we do about the meetings we scheduled?"
- "Why does this ERP vendor hate us?"

Our frustration fueled our determination. "How dare they cancel us. We're going to the conference anyway," we said.

I contacted the hotel receptionist. "I am glad you want them back. I've rebooked your rooms," she said.

Problem solved. Well, not really. The bigger issue was that the ERP vendor had canceled our conference passes, but, at this point, we didn't care. We were determined. We did not cancel any meetings. Instead, we planned to meet potential customers and partners outside the conference in the hotel lobby, bars, restaurants, or wherever we could make it work.

The Conference

In late September, when the poplar leaves are beginning to turn a vibrant, purplish red, and a few leaves have fluttered to the ground, we flew to the Nashville event as outsiders looking in. We had no passes and, therefore, no access to the exhibit area. So, when the breakout sessions wrapped and the attendees rushed to the lobby (exhibit area), our signature SourceDay green t-shirts and sport coats were nowhere to be seen.

But, thanks to the local hotel bars and restaurants, we met with a few partners and prospects. We made the most of a difficult situation. Resourcefulness and persistence matters when launching a start-up.

Day Two: My Entrepreneurial Mind Strikes Again

"Tom, what are the odds they remembered to cancel our conference badges? And, if they had, would they have remembered to remove them from the registration desk?" I asked as I chewed on the rubbery hotel eggs and sipped my morning Monster Energy drink during breakfast.

"Hmmm," he said, rubbing his chin, eyes gazing at the ceiling. He finished eating his cold, overcooked bacon and added, "We've never been ones to back down from a challenge. Let's find out."

Moments later, we were at the registration desk.

"Hello, we're here to pick up our badges," I said. I stated our names, and before you could say 'cool as a cucumber', we had pinned our badges to our shirts and were strutting around like our names were Clint and Tom Gaylord.

We now had full access to the conference, and, with chests fully puffed, we donned our bright green t-shirts and sport coats. By conference-end, we had talked to every partner and prospect that we had scheduled. We even struck up friendly conversations with team members of the ERP vendor that had blocked our attending the conference. In our minds, they were forgiven. Our experience ended up better because of the hardships we had endured.

It Gets Better

Our badges gave us full access to the Kelly Clarkson live performance. Tom and I had a grand time together at the concert.

> PERSPECTIVE: Because of our success as a company, in 2020 and 2021 we sponsored the Nashville conference and built more meaningful partnerships.

CHAPTER 5
THE BEST OF BOTH WORLDS

> **LESSSON LEARNED:**
> We are products of our environment.

> "The future influences the present just as much as the past."
> —Friedrich Nietzsche

My Dad

When cars were less reliable, before computerized everything, my father would come home from his job at McDermitt Engineering, change into his gray coveralls, motion to me with a tilt of his head, and go back to the garage where he had left his ailing vehicle. I always followed closely behind.

As was often the case, his car had developed a mechanical problem. While the engine was still hot, we would jack up the car and work, sometimes for hours, on the problem du jour until the car was repaired and ready to be driven safely to his office the next day.

Whether it be an oil change, replacing the brake pads, rebuilding carburetors, or something more involved like replacing the four-speed transmission, I cherished working with my father at our home in Houston under the hood or chassis of whatever vehicle he possessed at the time.

Without saying a word, my father would pass me a wrench, a screwdriver, a drill, or whatever tool was needed for the repair. We weren't aware of it at the time, but he was also passing to me his love of cars and his patience to make the needed repairs, whether it be on an automobile then or a start-up company now.

I recall one incident specifically:

"I'm home," Dad said as he took off his sports jacket and loosened his tie. For days and weeks we had been chasing an exhaust leak in his 1979 Firebird Formula.

"Dad, are we working on the car tonight?" I asked looking up from my algebra homework.

"Yep. Damn exhaust leak." Dad is a man of few words

Because my father's 1979 Firebird Formula had a 400-big block engine stuffed into it, there was little room to work. To repair the exhaust leak, we had to crawl under the car face up on the dirty concrete floor with flashlights in-hand and search for the problem. The good news? We knew where to find the leak. One of the exhaust manifold bolts had broken off. The bad news? It was nigh impossible to see and even harder to access.

Over the course of a week, we figured out how to get to the broken bolt, and then, once accessed, how to remove it.

We ended up using drills and Easy Out bits. In our case, it was anything but easy. We broke multiple bits before we finally succeeded in removing the bolt, replacing it, and sealing the exhaust leak. Any other human being would have said, "Take it to the dealership." But my father was determined to repair it ourselves in our garage. I'm pretty sure my never-give-up mindset came from this car repair episode.

> PERSPECTIVE: My dad can fix anything and build everything, whether it be a car or a dining room table. He learned that from his father, and now those skills have been passed down to me. Although, I believe that I have only learned about 30 or 40 percent of what he forgets every day.

My Love Affair

When I got my driver's license in 11th grade, my father gifted me his '79 Firebird Formula. He knew I had grown to love it, and he knew the Firebird symbolized something deeper. Working on that car together in the shadow of the dimly lit garage had forged an unbreakable bond between Dad and me; one that still exists today.

I knew every inch of that car: each spark plug, every radiator hose and clamp, the entire electrical system, and, yes, the exhaust manifold. And the love was not unrequited. The Firebird Formula and I spent many nights and weekends together on the unpatrolled Houston backroads.

What do I remember most about the car? It broke down a lot. On Saturday nights, when my friends were getting in all sorts of trouble, I was in our garage working on my car. In retrospect, I think I know exactly why dad offered me his cherished Firebird. He wanted to keep me doing something constructive, and he wanted to keep me out of trouble.

College Days and Beyond

I attended Stephen F. Austin State University for two years. My Firebird came with me. During summer break, I would return home to Houston and work at Slick 50, Inc., an engine treatment products company. Because I had worked with my dad and knew cars, I worked as the technical support, customer service agent. We would field technical questions about Slick 50: compatibility, benefits, longevity. I eventually became the manager.

Slick 50 had a great benefits package that included paying for my schooling if I promised to work there full-time. I took them up on their offer. Later, thanks to their funding, I graduated with a bachelor's degree in finance.

But it was now time to sell my beloved Firebird. I needed a reliable car to get me to work and to night school at the University of Houston. After a long goodbye, we parted our ways. Soon after, I bought a 1991 Nissan 300ZX Turbo. It too was fast and fun.

The Present

After I graduated from U of H, Dad bought a new fully loaded Corvette. I like to think he used my unused tuition money. These days, my dad is retired and doesn't fuss with car repairs, but he is always working on a project.

PART 2: CLINT MCCREE'S STORIES

As for me, I'm now looking for that 1979 Firebird with the 400-block engine. If I find it, I will restore it, and cherish it the rest of my life.

> PERSPECTIVE: There is a direct link between my career choices and working on cars with my dad. Whether it be an exhaust leak, engine additive advice, a mounted spotlight, launching a startup, or a supply chain dysfunction, it's about perseverance, it's about solving complex problems, and it's about loving what you do.

My Mom

Mom loves to tell this SourceDay-on-a-napkin story to her friends. I will retell it from my perspective:

Setting: Patio deck table

"Mom, I have an idea for a startup company," I said.

"What is the idea?" said Mom.

"My startup would help customers and their suppliers be more efficient."

"Show me. I need to visualize. I need to see a schematic."

Mom was an entrepreneur and had launched a few businesses of her own in the insurance field. Some were successful, some not so much. But she knew the difficulties, and she knew the rewards.

On the napkin nearest to me, I scribbled a schematic, showing the cloud as the missing link between supplier and customer.

"This is my idea for SourceDay—this is what I want to build."

Mom paused for a moment, rubbed her chin, looked at the sky and beyond and said, "Go for it."

My divorce was finalized in 2016. It was a difficult time for me. I was launching SourceDay with Tom, learning to be a single dad (which included the joy of coaching my sons on the weekends), and crafting the fine art of helping my oldest son through the ambivalent adventure of being recruited as a Division I athlete. I was essentially launching three start-ups simultaneously.

My mother was with me every step of the way. If I needed her to run an errand, drive one of my boys somewhere, cook us a meal, or process some legal issues, she was always there for me and her grandsons. Mom is a great listener and, when asked, offers sagacious advice. I am forever indebted.

"It's always dark before the sun comes up."
"Don't let divorce get in the way of your dreams."
"Don't lose sight of what you're building."
"You and Tom have something special at SourceDay."

Mom has always supported me. She is my rock.

PART 2: CLINT McCREE'S STORIES

The Apple Doesn't Fall...

My parents met at Boswell High School in Sagana, Texas. It's as stereotypical as it gets. My dad was the high school quarterback, and my mom was a cheerleader. After high school, my dad went on to college and got his master's in civil engineering. My mom went into the insurance industry.

My dad is introverted. My mom is the additive inverse. She is an extrovert who has never met a stranger she doesn't like; he or she will become an instant friend. She is the quintessential life of the party.

I live in both worlds, the perfect 50/50 only child. I can hold an engaging conversation with just about anyone, and I can fix their car. It's in my DNA.

PERSPECTIVE: I love my parents.

CHAPTER 6
THE ENIGMATIC CONNECTIVITY OF BEING ME

> **LESSSON LEARNED:**
> You can't go it alone when launching a start-up.

> "You spend a lot more time on your own as an only child. And there's space to allow your imagination to take flight."
> —Bill Bailey (English Actor, Comedian)

Latchkey Kid

I could have been the latchkey kid poster child. Both of my parents worked. I rode the bus, got dropped off at the top of the street, walked home, fed myself, did my homework, and went out and played with my friends. My parents came rolling in at 6:30 or 7:00. They never needed to worry. They knew I could take care of myself.

Only Child

When friends and colleagues find out that I am an only child, I usually get the same response, "That explains everything." One time, however, the response was a bit different (purposely written in present tense and only slightly exaggerated).

Our team is huddled around a conference table discussing a new iteration of our software. We take a break, agreeing to resume in 10. After a few minutes, a colleague returns, coffee cup in hand, and sits back down in her seat next to me. We begin a light conversation that soon turns to a discussion about family.

"Are your siblings entrepreneurial like you?" she asks as she takes a sip of her cappuccino.

I turn slightly in my leather, swivel chair and face her. "I'm an only child." I await the typical roll of the eyes, nod of the head, half-smile, and cliche: "That explains everything."

Instead, I am left with a combination of saliva and cappuccino dripping from my stoic face. Apparently, she had consumed more than a sip and, I discovered something else about my colleague, her spittle discharging skills are second to none.

"I'm so sorry," she says as she frantically tries to blot my face with the doily napkin that accompanied her cappuccino.

Was she sorry that she gave me an impromptu cappuccino shower, or was she sorry that I was an only child? I'll never know.

PART 2: CLINT MCCREE'S STORIES

An Only Child No More

I've read that only children are superior in character, achievement and intelligence. That may be true, but I couldn't have successfully launched SourceDay alone. I needed a kindred spirit who could offset my weaknesses and compliment my strengths. For example, I didn't know how to write software, or even where to begin. Tom filled that void perfectly. He had written and managed a team that had written software, and he had connections in the software world.

Tom took our business concepts and put them into developer speak. He worked with Mehedi (The Godfather), a developer who lived in Bangladesh (see Tom's Chapter 2). So, I dropped some cash into a holding account, we put a credit card down on a third-party website, and Mehedi began creating the software.

With Tom, I had a partner who was willing to go places that were incredibly difficult: no revenue, late hours, rejection. And he was persistent. I never questioned his work ethic or trustworthiness, and that is true to this day.

When we were further along in our startup journey, I remember telling my mom, "This guy gets it. I can trust him. I can count on him. If I'm going to war, Tom is the guy I want in the trenches with me."

Chief Operating Officer

In the early days of a start-up, titles are meaningless. The founders do everything. Tom and I were no exception. I did the selling and worked with consultants while Tom managed the product and the product development. He also presented demos to prospective clients. Together we on-boarded the suppliers and buyers when we sold to a new customer.

Because I had the idea for SourceDay, I was originally the CEO and Tom was the COO. But we quickly discovered that Tom was the better CEO fit, so we switched roles. This change didn't come easy for me, but, after some soul searching and some ego management, I realized it was the right decision.

For me, Tom is the perfect CEO. Why? Investors love him. He knows the analytics of our business down to the nth degree, and, because he knows the numbers, he can make fact-based assessments about SourceDay's future growth. He's also great at communicating the essence of SourceDay to current and future investors.

I have the COO title, and I'm still involved in all the departments but, mostly, I work forging alliances and partnerships with other organizations, some larger and some smaller than SourceDay. These partner relationships are valuable because they benefit our mutual customers and help us grow more rapidly.

While I work with larger strategic partners, I spend the majority of my time with "channel partners." What are channel partners? They are the link between the publisher of the ERP (Infor, Epicor, Microsoft, SAP, and Oracle) and the customer. They are a middle company that takes the publisher's ERP and resells it.

A channel partner also implements and supports the ERP for the customer. We partner with them because they are the trusted advisor to their customers and because they can resell our software to the same customers. Together we have a great story to tell.

> **PERSPECTIVE:** I'm not entirely sure how being a latchkey kid, an only child, a startup partner, and a COO all connect. Hence the word "enigmatic". But let me try.

Latchkey Kid: Learned to take care of myself and solve problems on my own.

Only Child: Because I had no siblings my parents could focus 100% on raising me. They taught me important life lessons that helped forge my character, and they promoted my education.

Startup Partner: I found the perfect partner in Tom. We bring out the best in each other.

COO: Leadership responsibilities reveal character. I think I'm doing okay.

I love what I do. I love hearing our customers' stories and helping them solve complex problems. I love working with our channel partners and helping them solve problems for their customers. The pain, the problems, and their solutions are what I love.

EPILOGUE

> "In the midst of winter, I found within me, an invincible summer. And that makes me happy. For it says that no matter how hard the world pushes against me, within me there's something stronger—something better pushing right back."
> —Albert Camus

When I wrote the original SourceDay Executive Summary in 2012, I had no idea that, eleven years later, I would be partnering with Tom to run a successful supply chain collaboration software company that prevents late part deliveries for manufacturers, wholesale distributors and retailers, by automating direct materials PO changes.

I did not anticipate the positive effect our software would have on our clients, their suppliers, and their families. I did not know that our start-up and investment partners would forge such beneficial, symbiotic relationships. And I did not consider that our employees would matter so much to me.

I hope our book reveals the complexities of launching a start-up. You really can't anticipate the setbacks and the failures associated with running a business until you get in the rocket ship and start your engines. But you can learn along the way.

Writing my SourceDay story has allowed me to reflect on the obstacles we have overcome, the milestones we have reached, and, most importantly, to appreciate the people who have helped us get to where SourceDay is today.

ABOUT TOM AND CLINT

Tom Kieley graduated from Texas A&M in 2004 and co-founded SourceDay in 2015 after launching his first tech startup, RG, in 2008. Earlier in his career, he started as a manufacturing supervisor at Dell and later transitioned into enterprise selling with software companies like Boomi and Pervasive.

Tom and his co-founder, Clint McRee, started SourceDay to transform how manufacturers, distributors, and retailers collaborate with their suppliers to solve the same supply chain challenges Tom and Clint experienced early in their careers. At the time of publishing, SourceDay has helped over 250 customers and 16,000 suppliers globally improve visibility and collaboration in their supply chains.

Tom is a husband, father of three, and exercise fanatic who loves cars, boating, and anything outdoors.

Clint McRee is a proud dad and, when his boys are on the gridiron, a football fan. Go Trojans and Westlake High School. He's a retired youth sports coach and loves a good adrenaline rush from sports, cars, racing and just about any competition.

He co-founded SourceDay in 2015 because he had supply chain issues. Realizing he had two career strengths, selling enterprise software and running a manufacturing company, he decided to combine them and chase his dream of being an entrepreneur and building a SaaS business from the ground up.

Clint joined forces with Tom to help companies suffering supply chain woes. He can't tell how many times he and Tom were told, 'You're crazy to build SourceDay.' He's glad he didn't follow their advice.